ANIMAL CLASSIFICATION

FISH

by
Steffi Cavell-Clarke

KidHaven
PUBLISHING

Published in 2017 by
KidHaven Publishing, an Imprint of Greenhaven Publishing, LLC
353 3rd Avenue
Suite 255
New York, NY 10010

Designer: Natalie Carr
Editor: Grace Jones

Cataloging-in-Publication Data
Names: Cavell-Clarke, Steffi.
Title: Fish / Steffi Cavell-Clarke.
Description: New York : KidHaven Publishing, 2017. | Series: Animal classification | Includes index.
Identifiers: ISBN 9781534520097 (pbk.) | ISBN 9781534520110 (library bound) | ISBN 9781534520103 (6 pack) | ISBN 9781534520127 (ebook)
Subjects: LCSH: Fishes–Juvenile literature.
Classification: LCC QL617.2 C38 2017 | DDC 597–dc23

Printed in the United States of America

CPSIA compliance information: Batch #CW17KL: For further information contact Greenhaven Publishing LLC, New York, New York at 1-844-317-7404.

Please visit our website, www.greenhavenpublishing.com. For a free color catalog of all our high-quality books, call toll free 1-844-317-7404 or fax 1-844-317-7405.

CONTENTS

Words that are underlined are explained in the glossary on page 31.

THE ANIMAL KINGDOM

The animal kingdom includes more than 8 million known living <u>species</u>. They come in many different shapes and sizes, they each do weird and wonderful things, and they live all over Earth.

From the freezing Arctic waters to the hottest desert in the world, animals have <u>adapted</u> to the often extreme and diverse conditions on Earth.

Even though each and every species of animal is unique, they still share certain characteristics with each other. These shared characteristics are used to classify animals. There are six main groups used to classify animals. They are mammals, reptiles, birds, insects, amphibians, and fish.

This shark is a fish.

FISH

WHAT IS A FISH?

A fish is a type of animal that has a <u>streamlined</u> body with a backbone, gills, and fins.

All fish must live in water to survive. Most fish are cold-blooded and covered in scales. However, there are a few exceptions! Overall, there are six characteristics that nearly all fish have in common.

Fish of the same species generally live together in large groups called schools.

There are more than 30,000 known species of fish alive today. Each species is different and has adapted in its own way to make it easier to survive in its habitat. Sharks, rays, eels, and salmon are all types of fish.

whale shark

The largest species of fish on Earth is the whale shark, which can grow up to 62 feet (19 m) long. The smallest family of fish in the world are the goby fish, which are just 0.3 inch (8 mm) long.

FISH CHECKLIST

 lives in water
has scales
breathes through gills
has fins
is cold-blooded
is a <u>vertebrate</u>

BODY PARTS

Even though all species of fish are unique, they can still be grouped together based on their similarities. There are three main groups of fish.

JAWLESS FISH

Jawless fish don't have <u>jaws</u>. Instead, they have sucker discs with tongues and small teeth.

CARTILAGINOUS FISH

Cartilaginous fish have skeletons that are made from a flexible tissue called <u>cartilage</u>.

BONY FISH

Bony fish have skeletons and swim bladders. Nearly 90 percent of all fish are bony fish.

FINS

Fish have several fins that help them move through water. These fins are also used for balance, as they help the fish keep straight and upright while swimming. The most important fin is the caudal fin, which is also known as the tail fin. Fish use their caudal fins to propel themselves through water.

pectoral fin

dorsal fin

caudal fin

gills

anal fin

SCALES

The skin of a fish is often covered in scales. Scales are overlapping pieces of bone-like material that form a protective layer around the fish's body. Scales can be round and smooth or pointed and rough. Fish scales are often covered in a layer of slime that helps the fish move through water easily.

Sharks are covered in tiny scales that make their skin tough like armor. These scales are called denticles and are shaped like curved, grooved teeth.

A shark's skin is rough like sandpaper!

SWIM BLADDER

Many fish have a swim bladder, which is an air-filled <u>organ</u> that helps fish stay afloat when they're not swimming. Cartilaginous fish don't have a swim bladder, which means they must keep swimming at all times or they will sink.

Goldfish are often kept as pets. If they're fed too much, their swim bladders may stop working, causing them to float to the surface of the water. When this happens, many people think their goldfish is dead when it only needs a change of diet to help it recover!

GETTING AROUND

Most fish get around by using their muscles and tail to swim through water. They use the muscles on the sides of their body to move their caudal fin from side to side, which pushes them forward. Fish that have fins on the sides of their body use them to steer and change direction. Rays have large, flat pectoral fins that gently rise up and down, which allows them to glide through water.

ray

The sailfish is the fastest swimming fish in the world. It can swim at a speed of **42 miles (68 km)** per hour.

All fish have gills that allow them to breathe underwater. Gills are organs that are generally located on each side of a fish's head. As water flows over the gills, oxygen passes into the fish's bloodstream.

gills

dolphin

Dolphins and whales need to swim to the water's surface to breathe. This is because they breathe with lungs, which means they're classified as mammals, not fish!

PREDATORS AND PREY

All animals can be sorted into groups depending on what they eat. The three groups are carnivores, herbivores, and omnivores.

herbivores
plant eaters

carnivores
meat eaters

omnivores
plant and meat eaters

Different types of fish belong to each group. Many fish eat live plants, while others eat dead plants found on the ocean floor. Carnivorous fish normally <u>prey</u> on insects and smaller fish. Omnivorous fish tend to eat plants and other dead animals, but they won't necessarily hunt live animals to eat.

Sharks are <u>predatory</u> carnivores, which means they hunt other animals for food. Sharks have several rows of triangular teeth along their jaws. When a shark loses a tooth, a new one replaces it. On average, a shark will lose and replace one tooth every seven or eight days. This makes their mouths perfect for catching and eating animals.

the jaws of a shark

Tiger sharks are **cannibals**! This means they eat other animals of the **same** species.

OCEANS, STREAMS, AND CORAL REEFS

Habitats can provide food and shelter for the animals and plants that live in them. Fish can be found in many habitats—from the world's largest oceans to small, fast-running streams. One of the main differences between habitats is the type of water the fish are swimming in. There's salt water, which is found in oceans and seas, and freshwater, which is found in lakes, rivers, streams, and ponds.

freshwater

salt water

Different species of fish are suited to different types of water. For example, goldfish are freshwater fish, which means they wouldn't be able to survive in the salty water of the ocean. However, there are some species of fish that can survive in both.

Coral reefs are home to many different species of fish. Coral reefs are found in warm, coastal waters in <u>tropical</u> regions of the world. They're excellent habitats for fish because they provide a rich food supply. Some fish also hide in coral reefs for protection against predators.

Clownfish live inside <u>venomous</u> corals to prevent predators from catching and eating them. Clownfish have adapted over time, and now venom doesn't affect them.

The largest **coral reef** is the Great Barrier Reef, which lies off the coast of northeastern **Australia.**

ADAPTATION

Fish have adapted to their environment in many ways. One of the most common fish adaptations is <u>camouflage</u>. Fish display a wide variety of colors and patterns that help them blend in with their environment.

Camouflage helps fish avoid being seen by predators, which means they're likely to survive longer. Some fish, such as the flatfish, can change their skin color to match the surrounding environment.

flatfish

Fish that live in **coral reefs** are often very **brightly colored** in order to **blend in** with the **colorful corals.**

When bony fish <u>reproduce</u>, they lay millions of eggs at one time. This is a special adaptation that only applies to bony fish. They do this because many eggs are eaten by other fish, and while the baby fish are still small they're easily snapped up by predators. The large number of eggs increases the chance some of the fish will survive until adulthood.

salmon eggs

LIFE CYCLES

A life cycle is the series of changes a living thing goes through from the start to the end of its life. Fish have developed many different ways to help their babies survive. Most fish lay eggs in water that hatch into tiny fish called fry. The parents generally don't stay with their babies, but they let them grow on their own.

There are other types of fish that carry their eggs within their body and give birth to babies. Some species of female sharks, such as hammerhead and basking sharks, give birth to baby sharks called

pups. Great white sharks are even born with a full set of teeth! These sharks are immediately ready to swim away from their mother and start hunting after they're born.

A male sea horse has a pouch on the front of his body that holds the eggs until they're ready to hatch.

LIFE CYCLE OF A SALMON

eggs

Salmon start and end their life cycle in a freshwater stream. A female salmon makes a nest on the bottom of a cold stream. She digs a hole with her tail in the gravel and lays hundreds of eggs. A male salmon will then <u>fertilize</u> them. The female hides the eggs by flicking gravel over them.

After six years, the salmon are fully grown. They swim back upstream to lay their eggs where they were hatched. After they lay them on the stream floor, they die. Their bodies float away and fill the stream with <u>nutrients</u> for the new baby salmon.

adulthood

fry

After 28 days, salmon fry hatch from the eggs.
They hide under gravel, safe from predators,
until they're strong enough to swim.

smolt

After a month, the fry push
their way out of the gravel
to find food. Within two
months, the young salmon,
called smolts, develop spots
and stripes, and they swim
downstream toward the sea.
Once they arrive, they feed
on shrimp and plankton.

EXTREME FISH

GREAT WHITE SHARK

All sharks are carnivores. They hunt and chase after their prey by moving through the water. The great white shark has developed very powerful senses that help it find its prey. It uses a unique sensor system located in its nose. This system means great white sharks detect the smallest movements in water, including fish lying under the sand!

Size:
21 feet
(6.4 m) long

Home:
coastal areas

Diet:
fish, rays,
seals, and
other sharks

OCEAN SUNFISH

Ocean sunfish are the heaviest bony fish in the world. They can weigh up to 2,200 pounds (1,000 kg)! They have a flat body with two long pectoral fins. They spend most of their time floating on the surface of tropical regions of the ocean to soak up the sun's rays. The female ocean sunfish can lay up to 300 million eggs at one time!

Size:
5 feet
(1.5 m) long

Home:
tropical parts
of the ocean

Diet:
jellyfish

PUFFER FISH

The puffer fish has an amazing way of protecting itself from predators. When the puffer fish is threatened, it blows up its body with air so it increases in size. Sharp spikes emerge all over its body to ward off predators.

The spikes are full of dangerous venom, too! Even though the puffer fish is one of the most poisonous animals in the world, people sometimes catch, cook, and serve them as a meal!

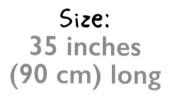

Size:
35 inches
(90 cm) long

Home:
tropical,
coastal waters

Diet:
algae and
shellfish

LEAFY SEA DRAGON

The leafy sea dragon gets its name from the flaps of skin all over its body. As it moves though water, the skin flaps drift behind it, which makes it look like floating seaweed. This form of camouflage helps the leafy sea dragon stay hidden as it drifts through open water. It also has a long, straw-like mouth for sucking up tiny shrimp.

Size:
9 inches
(24 cm) long

Home:
off the southern and western coasts of Australia

Diet:
shrimp, sea lice, and fry

FISH IN DANGER

The world's oceans are some of the most diverse environments, but they've become a dumping ground for waste created by people all over the world. Oil spills from ships <u>pollute</u> the water, which can destroy habitats and kill sea life.

Plastic garbage, such as grocery bags, is a major problem, as it doesn't break down like normal garbage and can stay in the water for many years. These different types of pollution have led to many species of fish becoming <u>endangered</u>.

To help prevent more fish from becoming endangered, people need to look after the seas, oceans, and freshwater habitats. Protecting the habitats of fish can help save many animals. People can do this by recycling all their waste correctly and never throwing garbage on the ground.

People around the world waste a huge amount of water every year, which can damage the world's natural habitats. We can all help by trying to save water every day.

FIND OUT MORE

BOOKS

Fish
by Grace Jones
(BookLife, 2016)

Fish: A Question and Answer Book
by Isabel Martin
(Capstone Press, 2016)

WEBSITES

BBC NATURE

www.bbc.co.uk/nature/animals/by/fish

Discover all the different species of fish and their habitats.

Great White Shark

kids.nationalgeographic.com/animals/
great-white-shark/#great-white-shark-
swimming-blue.jpg

National Geographic Kids features facts, videos, and interactive content about great white sharks.

GLOSSARY

adapted	changed over time to suit an environment
bloodstream	blood that circulates around the body
camouflage	colors, shapes, or patterns that help an animal hide in its environment
cartilage	a firm but flexible material that makes up the skeleton of some fish
endangered	when an animal or plant species is in danger of dying out
fertilize	to make an egg able to develop into a new living thing
jaws	bony structures that form the framework of the mouth and contain teeth
nutrients	substances that help plants and animals grow
organ	a part of the body that has a specific job
oxygen	a gas that animals need to breathe to stay alive
pollute	to add harmful things to the environment
predatory	referring to an animal that naturally preys on others
prey	to hunt other animals
reproduce	to produce new members of the same species
species	a group of very similar animals that are capable of producing babies together
streamlined	creating the least resistance to water and air
tropical	referring to warm and wet areas near the equator
unique	unlike anything else
venomous	an animal that can inject poison through a bite or sting
vertebrate	an animal with a backbone

INDEX